Dedication:
This book is dedicated to my daughter, Thyri, and my nephew, Tristan. You both endured the hardest parts of my parenting journey, and because of that, I'm able to share these lessons to help others. Thank you for your patience, resilience, and love. I love you more than words can express.

Not A Dr. Just A Mom

Become a Gentle Parent with Empathy Boundaries and Respect":

Not a Dr. Just a Mom is a heartfelt account by me, a single mother who has navigated countless challenges to arrive at this point in my life. Becoming a mother at 18, I faced the struggles of young parenthood without the guidance of an ideal upbringing. Growing up biracial and in financial hardship, I lacked a clear sense of identity, which shaped my journey. This book reflects my experiences of trial and error, embracing the individuality of every child while sharing the lessons I've learned along the way. More than just a memoir, it is a step-by-step guide for parents striving to cultivate gentleness and empathy in their parenting approach, providing actionable insights drawn from real-life challenges and triumphs.

By: Danielle Sylvester

What you will learn in this book

- Why gentle parenting matters
- Define gentle parenting: nurturing, empathetic, and respectful parenting that still enforces boundaries.
- Importance of balancing care and authority.
- Benefits for both parents and children: mutual trust, emotional intelligence, and conflict resolution skills.
- Navigating Conflict with Care
- Why Conflict Is an Opportunity for Growth
- Embracing Your Child's Unique Identity
- Why Acceptance Matters

Table of Contents for Not A Dr. Just A Mom: How to Become a Gentle Parent with Empathy, Boundaries, and Respect

1. Introduction: Why Gentle Parenting Matters
- Understanding empathy, respect, and boundaries in parenting

2. Setting the Foundation
- Defining your parenting philosophy
- Creating a parenting mission statement

3. Building a Strong Parent-Child Bond
- Connection before correction
- Active listening and daily rituals

4. Clear and Consistent Boundaries
- Communicating expectations
- Staying consistent but flexible
- Practical examples for setting boundaries

5. Handling Big Emotions
- Validating feelings, not actions
- Addressing tantrums with care
- Teaching emotional regulation

6. Teaching Accountability
- Using natural and logical consequences
- Encouraging problem-solving skills

7. Modeling Respect
- Demonstrating respectful communication
- Apologizing and self-regulation

8. Navigating Conflict with Care
- Viewing conflict as a growth opportunity
- Managing disagreements constructively

9. Creating a Harmonious Home
- Building a collaborative family environment
- Involving children in decisions
- Holding family meetings

10. Conclusion: Gentle Parenting Is a Journey
- Embracing imperfection in parenting
- The importance of self-care
- Encouragement for the journey ahead

Why Gentle Parenting Matters

Gentle parenting is more than a set of techniques—it's a mindset rooted in empathy, respect, and firm boundaries. In a world that often defaults to control and punishment, gentle parenting offers a transformative approach that prioritizes connection over correction. It acknowledges children as individuals with their own emotions, needs, and perspectives, fostering trust and cooperation rather than fear and compliance.

This book emphasizes gentle parenting because it equips parents with tools to nurture emotionally secure, confident, and empathetic children. By leading with compassion and modeling respect, parents create a foundation for lifelong relationships built on trust. Gentle parenting doesn't mean permissiveness or perfection—it means striving to understand your child while holding firm to values and boundaries that guide them with love.

This approach matters because it shapes not just how children behave today, but the kind of adults they become tomorrow. Every act of kindness, every boundary set with care, and every moment of empathy plants the seeds for a better future—for both your child and your relationship.

Chapter 1: Setting the Foundation

Understand Your Parenting Philosophy
- Reflect on your parenting values and goals.
- Align with the principles of gentle parenting: empathy, respect, and boundaries.
- Practical Exercise: Create a parenting mission statement.

Parenting is one of the most rewarding yet challenging roles we take on in life. Without a solid foundation, it can feel overwhelming to navigate the complex needs of raising a child while balancing your own emotions, responsibilities, and goals. The foundation of gentle parenting, grounded in empathy, respect, and firm boundaries, serves as your guiding framework, ensuring your approach is both nurturing and effective. Gentle parenting is not about being permissive or avoiding conflict; rather, it's about creating a safe and respectful environment where children learn through connection and understanding. Setting clear expectations and boundaries, while maintaining empathy and respect, helps foster trust, security, and cooperation.

Why the Foundation Matters

Imagine building a house without a blueprint. Each wall might stand on its own for a while, but without a strong structure, the house will eventually collapse under pressure. Similarly, parenting without a clear foundation can lead to confusion, inconsistency, and stress for both you and your child.

By establishing a clear parenting philosophy early on, you create consistency and predictability in your relationship with your child. They learn to trust that your words align with your actions, and they understand the boundaries within which they can safely explore, grow, and express themselves.

The principles of gentle parenting—empathy, respect, and boundaries—form the pillars of this foundation:
- Empathy teaches your child that their emotions are valid, even when their actions need guidance.
- Respect reinforces their self-worth while teaching them to value the feelings and perspectives of others.
- Boundaries provide structure, helping your child feel secure while understanding the limits of acceptable behavior.

A Real-Life Example: Conflict Resolution with My Daughter

When my daughter, Thyri, was around five years old, we had a conflict that could have easily escalated into frustration for both of us. It was bedtime, and she was refusing to put away her toys, claiming she wasn't tired and wanted to keep playing.

At first, I felt my patience wearing thin. I had a long day, and all I wanted was to get her to bed so I could have a moment to myself. But instead of reacting with anger or issuing a harsh command, I took a deep breath and reminded myself of the principles I wanted to follow: empathy, respect, and boundaries.

1. Empathy: I knelt down to her level and acknowledged her feelings. "I can see you're having so much fun with your toys, and it's hard to stop when you're really enjoying something."

2. Respect: I gave her space to share her thoughts without interrupting. "Can you tell me what you're feeling right now? Is there a way we can work together to end the night on a happy note?"

3. Boundaries: I calmly explained why bedtime was important and why the toys needed to be put away. "We have a routine because your body needs rest to grow strong and healthy, and we always clean up so we don't lose any of your favorite toys."

Instead of demanding she put the toys away, I offered her a choice. "Would you like to put the toys away now, or should we set a timer for five more minutes of play before cleanup?" She chose the timer, and when it went off, we worked together to tidy up.

By sticking to the principles of gentle parenting, I avoided a power struggle, validated her feelings, and still held the boundary of bedtime. That night, as I tucked her in, she hugged me and said, "Thank you for letting me play a little longer."

Building Your Foundation

To set the foundation for gentle parenting in your own home:

1. Clarify Your Values: Reflect on what matters most to you as a parent. Is it raising a kind, independent, or resilient child? Write down your parenting goals and the values you want to model.
2. Establish Boundaries: Clearly define the non-negotiables in your household. For example, bedtime routines, safety rules, or how family members communicate with each other.
3. Practice Empathy: Make it a habit to see situations from your child's perspective, even when they're testing boundaries. Empathy helps diffuse tension and opens the door for cooperation.
4. Stay Consistent: Children thrive on predictability. Follow through on what you say, and avoid empty threats or inconsistent rules.

The Importance of Intentional Parenting

Setting a strong foundation allows you to parent intentionally rather than reactively. When you understand your parenting philosophy and apply it consistently, you become a steady anchor for your child, even in moments of conflict. Your empathy shows them their emotions are valid, your respect teaches them self-worth, and your boundaries provide the structure they need to feel secure.

As you begin your journey with gentle parenting, remember: it's not about perfection but about progress. By focusing on building a strong foundation, you're not only guiding your child's growth but also strengthening the bond that will carry you through life's challenges together.

Practical Exercise: Create Your Parenting Mission Statement

A parenting mission statement is a guiding document that defines your values, goals, and approach to parenting. It helps you stay intentional in your decisions, especially during challenging moments. Follow these steps to create a mission statement that reflects gentle parenting principles with firm boundaries, respect, and empathy.

Step 1: Reflect on Your Parenting Values

Take a few moments to answer these questions:

- What qualities do I want to foster in my child (e.g., kindness, resilience, independence)?
- What kind of parent do I want to be (e.g., calm, supportive, consistent)?
- How do I want my child to feel when they interact with me (e.g., loved, safe, understood)?

Write down 3-5 core values that are most important to you. For example:
- Empathy
- Respect
- Growth

Step 2: Define Your Parenting Goals

Think about what you want to achieve as a parent in both the short and long term:

- Short-term: How do you want to handle daily conflicts and challenges?
- Long-term: What kind of relationship do you want with your child as they grow older?

Example:

- Short-term goal: To approach conflict calmly while maintaining clear boundaries.
- Long-term goal: To build a lifelong relationship based on mutual trust and respect.

Step 3: Integrate Gentle Parenting Principles

Consider how empathy, respect, and firm boundaries fit into your parenting philosophy. Ask yourself:

- How can I show empathy when my child is struggling?
- How do I model respect for my child while teaching them to respect others?
- How do I establish and maintain firm boundaries in a compassionate way?

Write down 1-2 examples for each principle to solidify your understanding.

Step 4: Draft Your Mission Statement

Use your reflections to craft a concise statement that reflects your parenting philosophy. Your mission statement should inspire and ground you during tough parenting moments.

Example Mission Statement:

"I strive to parent with empathy, respect, and understanding, fostering a safe and supportive environment where my child can grow into a kind, confident, and independent individual. I will set clear and consistent boundaries with love and patience, teaching my child how to navigate life's challenges while strengthening our relationship through connection and trust."

Step 5: Put It Into Practice
- Write your mission statement somewhere visible (e.g., a notebook, journal, or family board).
- Reflect on it when making parenting decisions, especially during conflicts.
- Revisit and revise it as your child grows or your values evolve.

By crafting and using your parenting mission statement, you'll have a steady reminder of your goals and values, helping you stay aligned with the principles of gentle parenting even in challenging moments.

Chapter 2: The Power of Connection

Build a Strong Parent-Child Bond
• Importance of connecting before correcting.
• Techniques for connection:
• Active listening.
• Daily check-ins.
• Practical Tips: 5-minute bonding rituals (e.g., bedtime chats, playful moments).

Building a Strong Parent-Child Bond
Parenting is not just about guiding behavior—it's about building a deep, meaningful connection with your child. A strong parent-child bond creates the foundation for trust, cooperation, and emotional resilience. When children feel deeply connected to their caregivers, they are more likely to listen, respect boundaries, and develop healthy self-esteem.
In gentle parenting, connection is the cornerstone of discipline. Before you correct or guide your child's behavior, it's essential to strengthen the bond that keeps your relationship steady, even during challenging moments.

Why Connection Matters Before Correction
Children thrive on connection. When they feel seen, heard, and valued, they are more likely to cooperate and less likely to engage in defiant or disruptive behavior. Correcting a child without connection can lead to power struggles, resentment, or feelings of inadequacy.

Connection before correction communicates:
• Empathy: "I understand how you're feeling."
• Respect: "I value you as a person."
• Safety: "Even when we disagree, our relationship is secure."

For example, if your child throws a tantrum over not getting a toy, leading with connection might look like:
1. Getting down to their eye level.
2. Saying, "I see you're really upset because you wanted that toy. It's hard when we can't have what we want."
3. After calming them, explaining the boundary: "We're not buying the toy today, but we can put it on your wish list."

This approach doesn't dismiss their feelings or compromise your boundaries—it balances empathy with guidance.

Techniques for Building Connection

1. Active Listening

- What It Is: Giving your full attention to your child when they're speaking or expressing themselves.
- Why It Matters: Active listening helps children feel understood and valued, which strengthens trust.
- **How to Do It:**
  - Maintain eye contact and put away distractions (like your phone).
  - Repeat back what you hear to show understanding: "You're upset because your friend didn't share with you. That must have been frustrating."
  - Avoid interrupting or jumping to solutions.

2. Daily Check-Ins

- What It Is: Taking time each day to connect one-on-one with your child.
- Why It Matters: Regular check-ins build emotional security and keep lines of communication open.
- **How to Do It:**
  - Ask open-ended questions: "What was the best part of your day? What was hard today?"
  - Share something about your own day to model openness.
  - Use this time to focus on your child without distractions.

3. 5-Minute Bonding Rituals

- What It Is: Short, intentional moments of connection that fit into your daily routine.
- Why It Matters: Even brief, consistent moments of bonding show your child they are a priority.
- *Examples*:
  - Bedtime Chats: Spend 5 minutes talking about their day, their dreams, or what they're looking forward to.
  - Playful Moments: Engage in a quick game, a silly dance, or a tickle session to lighten the mood.
  - Hugs and Affirmations: Start the day with a warm hug and a positive statement: "I'm so proud of you. You're going to do great today."

PRACTICAL EXAMPLE: CONNECTION IN ACTION

One evening, my daughter Thyri was upset because I asked her to turn off the TV and get ready for bed. Instead of immediately enforcing the rule, I chose to connect first.

1. I got down to her level and acknowledged her feelings: "You're upset because you want to keep watching your show. I get it—it's hard to stop when you're having fun."
2. I listened as she explained she was watching her favorite part of the episode.
3. I set the boundary with kindness: "I understand. How about we finish this episode tomorrow? Right now, it's bedtime because your body needs rest to grow strong."
4. We added a bonding moment: I offered to read an extra bedtime story as a way to connect before she drifted off to sleep.

By focusing on connection first, I diffused the situation, upheld the boundary, and ended the evening on a positive note.

Tips for Strengthening the Parent-Child Bond

- Be Present: Show your child that they are your priority by giving them undivided attention, even for a few minutes a day.
- Validate Their Feelings: Let them know their emotions are okay, even when their actions need guidance.
- Use Physical Affection: Hugs, pats on the back, or holding hands can go a long way in fostering connection.
- Apologize When Needed: If you lose your temper, model accountability by saying, "I'm sorry for yelling earlier. That wasn't okay."

The Power of Connection

Building a strong parent-child bond takes time, patience, and intentional effort, but the rewards are immeasurable. When your child feels connected to you, they are more likely to trust your guidance, respect your boundaries, and grow into a confident, compassionate individual.

Connection doesn't mean perfection. There will be tough days, but every moment spent listening, hugging, and empathizing strengthens the foundation of your relationship. Lead with love, follow with guidance, and watch your bond grow deeper each day.

Chapter 3: Clear and Consistent Boundaries

Be Clear About Expectations
• Communicating rules in an age-appropriate way.
• Examples: "We sit while we eat" instead of "Don't stand on the chair."
• Using visuals or charts for younger children.

Stay Consistent but Flexible
• Why consistency builds trust.
• When and how to adapt boundaries based on changing needs.

Part One

Boundaries are a cornerstone of gentle parenting. They provide children with a sense of security, structure, and understanding, helping them navigate the world with confidence. Clear and consistent boundaries are not about controlling your child; they are about guiding them toward appropriate behavior in a way that fosters respect and trust.

As a gentle parent, boundaries should be communicated with empathy, respect, and clarity, ensuring your child understands what is expected without feeling dismissed or shamed. This chapter will explore how to set boundaries in a way that supports your child's growth while maintaining harmony in your relationship.

Why Clear Boundaries Are Essential

Children thrive in environments where expectations are clear and consistent. Ambiguous or inconsistent boundaries can lead to confusion, frustration, and power struggles. By setting clear boundaries, you provide:

• Structure: Children know what to expect, which reduces anxiety and uncertainty.
• Safety: Boundaries help protect children from harm, teaching them what is acceptable and what isn't.
• Respect: When boundaries are communicated kindly and consistently, children learn to respect both the rules and the people enforcing them.

Be Clear About Expectations

One of the most important aspects of setting boundaries is clarity. Children, especially younger ones, respond better to simple, positive, and direct instructions. Instead of focusing on what they shouldn't do, emphasize what they should do.

Age-Appropriate Communication

- Toddlers and Preschoolers: Use short, simple sentences and clear visuals. *Example*: "We walk inside the house" instead of "Don't run!"
- School-Aged Children: Explain the "why" behind the rule to help them understand the reasoning. Example: "We clean up our toys so no one trips and gets hurt."
- Teens: Encourage open dialogue and involve them in setting boundaries. *Example*: "I trust you to hang out with friends, but let's agree on a curfew that works for both of us."

Positive Framing

Children respond better to instructions that focus on what they can do rather than what they can't.

- Instead of: "Don't stand on the chair!"
- Say: "We sit while we eat to stay safe."

Use Visuals or Charts for Younger Children

Visual aids can help young children understand and remember rules.

- *Examples*:
- A poster with illustrations of daily routines (e.g., brushing teeth, bedtime).
- A "house rules" chart with simple drawings (e.g., hands to ourselves, gentle voices).
- Involve your child in creating the visuals. This helps them feel invested in the rules and more likely to follow them.

How to Maintain Consistency

Consistency is key to reinforcing boundaries. When rules are applied predictably, children are less likely to test limits because they understand the outcomes.

1. Be Firm, Not Harsh
- Approach boundaries with kindness but remain unwavering in their enforcement.
- *Example*: If the rule is "We put away our toys before dinner," calmly remind your child and help them follow through instead of letting it slide one day and enforcing it the next.

2. Follow Through on Consequences
- Ensure that consequences are logical and connected to the behavior.
- *Example*: If your child refuses to put away their toys, the toys are temporarily unavailable until cleanup happens.

3. Model the Behavior You Expect
- Children learn by observing. If you want them to speak respectfully or clean up after themselves, demonstrate these behaviors consistently.

Practical Example: Setting Clear Boundaries at Mealtime

When my daughter Thyri was three, she often stood on her chair during meals, which was both distracting and unsafe. Initially, I found myself saying, "Don't stand on your chair!" repeatedly, only for her to do it again. I realized my approach wasn't clear or effective.

Here's how I adjusted using gentle parenting principles:
1. Clarity: I reframed the rule positively: "We sit while we eat to stay safe."
2. Consistency: Every time she started to stand, I calmly reminded her of the rule without raising my voice.
3. Respect: I acknowledged her feelings: "It's hard to sit still sometimes, isn't it? But we need to stay seated while we eat."
4. Engagement: To make sitting more fun, I introduced a silly game where she could "pretend to glue her bottom to the chair" before each meal.

By staying clear, calm, and consistent, the behavior changed over time without power struggles or frustration.

Tips for Setting Clear and Consistent Boundaries
- Start Small: Focus on a few essential rules at a time, especially for younger children.
- Be Realistic: Ensure boundaries are age-appropriate and achievable for your child's developmental stage.
- Acknowledge Success: Praise your child when they follow rules. For example, "Great job sitting so nicely at the table!"
- Stay Patient: Change doesn't happen overnight. Be consistent and patient as your child learns.

Part Two
Clear and Consistent Boundaries

Boundaries are essential in parenting. They help children understand expectations, develop self-regulation, and feel secure. However, boundaries alone are not enough—they need to be clear, consistent, and flexible to adapt to your child's evolving needs. This chapter explores how to set boundaries that balance structure and empathy while maintaining trust and respect.

Why Consistency Builds Trust

Consistency is the backbone of effective boundaries. When children know what to expect, they feel safe and secure. Inconsistent boundaries—enforcing a rule one day but ignoring it the next—can lead to confusion, frustration, and testing of limits.

Consistency communicates to your child:

- Reliability: "My parent means what they say, and I can trust their guidance."
- Fairness: "The rules apply equally and don't change based on their mood."
- Security: "I know what's expected of me and how to navigate my environment."

For example, if bedtime is at 8:00 p.m., enforcing that boundary consisteantly helps your child understand the routine. If bedtime is flexible one night but strictly enforced the next, your child may push back, unsure of the expectations.

While consistency is key, it's also important to remain flexible as your child grows and their needs evolve. Boundaries that worked for a toddler may not suit a school-aged child or teenager. Adapting boundaries when appropriate shows respect for your child's development and individuality.

Signs It's Time to Adjust a Boundary

- Developmental Growth: Your child has gained new skills or understanding that make the rule outdated.
- *Example*: Allowing an older child to stay up 30 minutes later because they no longer need as much sleep.
- Emotional Needs: The boundary is causing undue stress or frustration without a clear purpose.
- *Example*: Adjusting the rule for quiet time if your child finds it too long for their attention span.
- Situational Changes: A family change, like moving or starting a new school, may require flexibility to accommodate new routines.

How to Adapt Boundaries Effectively

1. Communicate the Change: Explain why the boundary is being adjusted in a way your child can understand.
- *Example*: "You've been doing a great job finishing your homework on time, so you can now decide whether to play before or after dinner."
2. Involve Your Child: When appropriate, include them in the decision-making process.
- *Example*: "You're growing up, so let's decide together what your new screen time rules should be."
3. Monitor the Change: Observe how the adjustment impacts your child's behavior and well-being, and be prepared to revisit it if needed.

Practical Example: Consistency with Flexibility
When my daughter, Thyri, was younger, we had a strict rule about screen time—30 minutes a day, no exceptions. This worked well when she was four or five, but as she grew older, she began using screens for educational games and schoolwork.

I realized the boundary needed to adapt to her changing needs, so I approached her with empathy and respect:

1. Acknowledged the Change: "You're using screens for more than just fun now, and I see that some days you need more time for schoolwork or creative projects."
2. Involved Her in the Process: "Let's set a new rule together. How much screen time do you think is reasonable for school days and weekends?"
3. Set a Clear New Boundary: Together, we decided on an hour for school days and two hours on weekends, with a focus on balance and breaks.

By adapting the rule while maintaining consistency in how it was communicated and enforced, we avoided power struggles and strengthened our trust.

Practical Tips for Staying Consistent Yet Flexible

- Stick to Core Values: While specific rules may change, the principles behind them—like respect, safety, and balance—should remain consistent.
- Use "When, Then" Statements: Create predictability while offering flexibility.
  - Example: "When you finish your chores, then you can have screen time."
- Reassess Regularly: Schedule periodic check-ins with yourself and your child to evaluate if boundaries are still effective and appropriate.
  - Ask yourself: "Is this rule meeting my child's current needs?"
  - Ask your child: "How do you feel about this rule? Do we need to adjust it?"
- Be Open to Feedback: Encourage your child to share their thoughts about boundaries.
  - **Example**: "I know you feel bedtime is too early. Let's talk about why it's important and see if there's room for adjustment."

Balancing Firmness with Flexibility

Consistency builds trust, but flexibility fosters growth. Together, they create a parenting approach that is both firm and compassionate. By staying consistent in your core values and flexible in your methods, you teach your child that rules are not arbitrary—they are tools to guide them toward independence and self-regulation.

As you practice setting clear and consistent boundaries, remember: gentle parenting is about creating a relationship built on trust, empathy, and respect. Boundaries are not barriers; they are bridges that help you and your child navigate life's challenges together.

Chapter 4: Handling Big Emotions

Validate Feelings, Not Actions
 • Teaching children to name and process emotions.
 • Example: "I see you're upset because you can't have the toy right now. It's okay to feel sad."

Temper Tantrums: Addressing with Care
 -Steps for managing tantrums:
 -Stay calm.
 -Get on their level.
 -Offer comfort while holding the boundary.
 -Examples of what to say:
 -"I'm here, but throwing toys is not okay."

Children experience emotions with an intensity that can sometimes feel overwhelming—for them and for us as parents. Whether it's a tantrum in the grocery store or tears over a lost toy, these moments are a natural part of growing up. However, how we respond as parents can profoundly shape how our children learn to manage their emotions over time.

In gentle parenting, the focus is not on suppressing emotions or avoiding difficult moments but on helping children understand, name, and process their feelings. This approach requires empathy, respect, and firm boundaries, balancing validation of emotions with guidance on acceptable actions.

When children express big emotions, it's tempting to focus on stopping the behavior—yelling, crying, or hitting. However, addressing the emotion behind the action is far more effective. By validating your child's feelings, you show them that emotions are natural and acceptable, even if their actions need redirection.

Children are emotional beings, and as they grow, they often struggle to understand and manage the intensity of their feelings. Whether it's sadness, anger, or frustration, big emotions are a natural part of their development. For parents practicing gentle parenting, these moments are not just challenges but opportunities to teach empathy, self-regulation, and respect.

One of the most common expressions of big emotions in children is the temper tantrum. This chapter will explore how to validate feelings while maintaining boundaries, and how to address tantrums with care, ensuring that both your child and your relationship emerge stronger from these moments.

Validation teaches your child:
- Self-Awareness: Naming emotions helps them understand what they're feeling.
- Emotional Regulation: Acknowledging feelings creates space for calm problem-solving.
- Empathy: When their emotions are respected, they learn to respect others' feelings too.

Key Principle: "Feelings are always okay. Certain actions are not."

For example:
- Feeling: It's okay to feel angry when your block tower falls.
- Action: Throwing blocks at others is not okay.

Teaching Children to Name and Process Emotions

Helping children identify and understand their emotions is a foundational skill for emotional intelligence. Here's how to guide them:

1. Label the Emotion:
- Use simple language to help them identify their feelings.
- Example: "You're feeling frustrated because the puzzle piece doesn't fit."
- For younger children, use visual aids like emotion charts with faces showing different feelings.

2. Acknowledge the Cause:
- Reflect on what triggered the emotion without judgment.
- Example: "I see you're upset because you can't have the toy right now. It's okay to feel sad."

3. Normalize the Emotion:
- Reassure your child that it's normal to feel that way.
- Example: "It's hard to not get what we want sometimes. Everyone feels like that."

4. Offer a Coping Strategy:
- Teach them ways to process emotions in a healthy way.
- ***Examples***:
  - Take deep breaths together.
  - Hug a favorite stuffed animal.
  - Draw or write about their feelings.

Practical Example: Validating Feelings in Action

One afternoon, my daughter Thyri became upset when I told her she couldn't have a cookie before dinner. She started crying loudly and stomping her feet, clearly overwhelmed by disappointment.

Here's how I applied the principles of gentle parenting:

1. Validated Her Feelings:
- I knelt down to her level and calmly said, "I can see you're really upset because you wanted that cookie. It's hard to wait, isn't it?"

2. Set the Boundary:
- I gently reminded her, "We don't have cookies before dinner because we need to save room for healthy food."

3. Offered Support:
- I held her hand and said, "It's okay to feel sad. Let's think about something fun we can do while we wait for dinner."

4. Redirected Her Energy:
- We decided to color together until it was time to eat. This gave her a positive outlet for her emotions.

By validating her feelings and maintaining the boundary, I helped her process her disappointment without giving in or dismissing her emotions.

Tips for Handling Big Emotions
- **Stay Calm:** Your reaction sets the tone. Take a deep breath before responding to ensure you approach the situation with empathy.
- **Use Empathy Statements:**
  - "I understand why you're feeling this way."
  - "It's okay to be upset. I'm here to help you."
- **Redirect Actions:** While validating emotions, calmly guide your child toward appropriate behaviors.
- ***Example***: "It's okay to feel mad, but we don't hit. Let's use our words to tell me how you feel."
- **Teach Self-Regulation Over Time:** As your child grows, introduce strategies like taking a break, journaling, or practicing mindfulness to help them manage their emotions independently.

The Long-Term Impact of Validation

When you validate your child's feelings, you teach them that emotions are not something to fear or suppress. Instead, they learn to process their feelings in a healthy, constructive way. Over time, this builds their emotional resilience and strengthens your bond.

Handling big emotions with empathy, respect, and boundaries doesn't mean letting your child do whatever they want—it means creating a safe space for them to express themselves while learning what is and isn't acceptable.

By practicing these techniques, you're equipping your child with the tools they need to navigate their emotions confidently and respectfully, setting them up for a lifetime of healthy relationships and self-awareness.

Validating Feelings, Not Actions

When your child experiences big emotions, their actions may not always align with acceptable behavior. While it's important to hold firm boundaries, it's equally vital to validate their feelings. This teaches your child that all emotions are okay, even when certain actions are not.

How to Validate Feelings:
1. Name the Emotion: Help your child identify what they're feeling.
- *Example*: "You're feeling angry because your block tower fell over."
2. Acknowledge the Cause: Let them know you understand why they feel this way.
- *Example*: "It's really frustrating when things don't work out the way we want."
3. Normalize the Emotion: Reassure them that it's okay to feel what they're feeling.
- *Example*: "It's okay to feel upset. Everyone feels that way sometimes."

Important Reminder: While you validate their feelings, make it clear that not all actions are acceptable.
- *Example*: "It's okay to feel angry, but we don't throw toys. Let's find another way to show how you feel."

Temper Tantrums: Addressing with Care
Temper tantrums are a normal part of childhood. They often occur when a child is overwhelmed by feelings they can't yet express or control. Handling tantrums with care requires patience, empathy, and a commitment to maintaining boundaries.

Steps for Managing Tantrums
1. Stay Calm:
- Your child's tantrum is not a personal attack—it's their way of expressing overwhelming emotions.
- Take a deep breath and remind yourself that your calmness sets the tone for the interaction.
2. Get on Their Level:
- Physically kneel or sit so you are at eye level with your child. This conveys empathy and helps them feel heard.
- Avoid standing over them, as this can feel intimidating.
3. Offer Comfort While Holding the Boundary:
- Provide reassurance that you're there to help them through their feelings.
- Calmly remind them of the boundary they've crossed.
- *Example*: "I'm here, but throwing toys is not okay. Let's put the toys down and take a deep breath together."

Examples of What to Say During a Tantrum
- Acknowledging Feelings:
- "I see you're really upset because we have to leave the park. It's hard to stop having fun."
- Setting Boundaries:
- "I'm here to help, but hitting is not okay. Let's use our words instead."
- Offering Comfort:
- "It's okay to feel sad. I'll stay with you until you're ready to talk."

Practical Example: Handling a Grocery Store Tantrum
One day, my daughter Thyri had a meltdown in the grocery store when I said no to buying candy. She cried loudly and sat on the floor, refusing to move.

Here's how I managed the situation using the steps above:

1. Stayed Calm:
- I took a deep breath and reminded myself that tantrums are normal.

2. Got on Her Level:
- I knelt down and made eye contact.

3. Validated Her Feelings:
- "You're really upset because I said no to the candy. I understand—it's disappointing."

4. Held the Boundary:
- "We're not buying candy today, but we can add it to our list for a special treat another time."

5. Offered Comfort:
- "It's okay to feel sad. Let's take a moment here, and when you're ready, we can keep shopping together."

After a few minutes, she calmed down enough to continue. By staying calm and addressing her feelings while holding the boundary, we avoided escalating the situation.

Tips for Addressing Tantrums with Care

- Avoid Escalation: Respond with calm, not frustration. If you yell or threaten, it can intensify the tantrum.
- Be Present: Let your child know they're not alone in their feelings. Sometimes just sitting quietly nearby is enough.
- Redirect When Appropriate: Once your child is calmer, gently shift their attention to something else.
- Revisit Later: After the tantrum has passed, talk about it calmly to reinforce boundaries and discuss better ways to handle similar feelings in the future.

Final Thoughts

Handling big emotions and temper tantrums with empathy, respect, and boundaries helps children learn that all feelings are valid, but not all actions are acceptable. By staying calm, validating their feelings, and maintaining consistent boundaries, you're teaching them how to navigate their emotions in a healthy, constructive way.

These moments, while challenging, are opportunities to deepen your bond and equip your child with lifelong emotional regulation skills. As you guide them through their big emotions, remember: gentle parenting is not about perfection, but about connection, growth, and mutual respect.

Chapter 5: Teaching Accountability

Use Natural and Logical Consequences
• Difference between punishments and consequences.
• *Example*: If a child refuses to wear a coat, let them experience the cold briefly (natural consequence).
-Teach Problem-Solving Skills
• Encourage children to participate in finding solutions.
• *Example*: "You don't want to clean your toys. What do you think we can do to make it easier?"

One of the most valuable life skills we can teach our children is accountability. It's the foundation of responsibility, independence, and problem-solving. Accountability doesn't come from punishments or fear—it comes from understanding the impact of one's actions and learning how to make better choices in the future.
In gentle parenting, accountability is taught through empathy, respect, and consistent boundaries. By using natural and logical consequences and involving children in problem-solving, we empower them to take ownership of their actions in a way that fosters growth, rather than guilt or shame.
Natural and Logical Consequences
Consequences are a powerful tool in teaching accountability, but they must be used thoughtfully. Unlike punishments, which are designed to control behavior through fear or discomfort, consequences help children connect their actions to real-world outcomes.

Difference Between Punishments and Consequences
• Punishment: Often unrelated to the behavior and rooted in control or retribution.
• Example: A child spills juice and is sent to their room as punishment.
• Consequence: A natural or logical result of the behavior that teaches responsibility.
• *Example*: A child spills juice and is asked to help clean it up.

Natural Consequences
Natural consequences occur without parental intervention and are directly tied to the child's choices.
• *Example*: If a child refuses to wear a coat on a chilly day, they will feel cold. This teaches them the importance of dressing appropriately without needing a lecture or punishment.

Guidelines for Using Natural Consequences:

1. Ensure the consequence is safe and not harmful.
2. Allow the experience to unfold without stepping in to rescue or criticize.
3. Use empathy to help the child process the outcome.

- What to Say:
- "You didn't want to wear your coat, and now you're feeling cold. Let's remember this next time so you can stay warm."

Logical Consequences

Logical consequences are set by parents and are directly related to the child's behavior.

- **Example**: If a child refuses to put away their toys, the toys may be temporarily put away where they cannot play with them until cleanup is done.

Guidelines for Using Logical Consequences:

1. Make sure the consequence is fair and related to the behavior.
2. **Explain** the connection between the behavior and the consequence.
3. Deliver the consequence calmly and respectfully.

- What to Say:
- "We need to take care of our toys. Since they weren't cleaned up, they'll take a break for now. You can play with them again after we tidy up."

Teaching Problem-Solving Skills

Accountability isn't just about consequences; it's also about equipping children with the tools to solve problems and make better choices. By involving children in the process of finding solutions, you encourage critical thinking, creativity, and responsibility.

How to Encourage Problem-Solving

1. Identify the Problem Together:
- Help your child articulate the issue without judgment.
- **Example**: "You don't want to clean up your toys. Can you tell me why?"

2. Brainstorm Solutions:
- Invite your child to share their ideas for solving the problem. Offer guidance if needed.
- **Example**: "What do you think we can do to make cleanup easier?"
- Their suggestion might be to turn cleanup into a game or to do it together.

3. Agree on a Plan:
- Choose a solution together and clearly outline what will happen next.
- **Example**: "Okay, let's race to see how quickly we can clean up. I'll help you with the blocks while you take care of the cars."

4. Follow Through:
- Ensure the agreed-upon solution is implemented and acknowledge their effort.
- Example: "Great job cleaning up! It feels good to have a tidy space, doesn't it?"

Practical Example: Accountability in Action

One evening, my daughter Thyri didn't want to clean up her art supplies after craft time. Instead of demanding she clean up or scolding her for refusing, I approached the situation with gentle parenting principles.

1. Identified the Problem:
• "It looks like you're feeling tired of cleaning up. Is that right?"
2. Explored the Natural Consequence:
• "If we leave the markers out, they might dry up, and we won't be able to use them again. What do you think about that?"
3. Brainstormed a Solution:
• She suggested, "Maybe we can do it together?"
4. Followed Through with Empathy:
• We cleaned up together, and I praised her for taking responsibility. "Thank you for helping! Now your markers will be ready for next time."

By involving her in the problem-solving process, I helped her see the connection between her actions and the outcome, without resorting to threats or punishments.

Tips for Teaching Accountability
• Stay Calm: Focus on the lesson, not the mistake. Avoid lecturing or shaming.
• Use "When, Then" Statements: Link actions to outcomes in a clear and respectful way.
• **Example**: "When your homework is done, then you can play your game."
• Acknowledge Effort: Celebrate when your child takes responsibility or comes up with a solution.
• Example: "I noticed you cleaned up without me asking—great job taking care of your space!"
• Be Patient: Learning accountability is a gradual process. Allow your child to make mistakes and learn from them.

Final Thoughts

Teaching accountability through natural and logical consequences and problem-solving skills empowers children to take ownership of their actions in a way that is respectful and constructive. Instead of fearing punishment, they learn to understand the impact of their choices and develop the tools to make better decisions.

As you guide your child through these lessons, remember that accountability is not about perfection—it's about growth. By fostering a culture of empathy, respect, and clear boundaries, you're equipping your child with the skills they need to navigate life with confidence and responsibility.

Chapter 6: Modeling Respect

Be a Role Model
- Children learn respect through observation.
- Demonstrate respectful communication and self-regulation.
- Examples: Apologizing when you're wrong, managing your emotions calmly.

Children are like sponges—they absorb the behaviors, language, and attitudes of the people around them, especially their parents. If we want to raise respectful children, we must first model respect ourselves. Respect is not something we demand; it's something we demonstrate.
In gentle parenting, respect begins with how we treat our children. When they experience empathy, kindness, and fairness firsthand, they learn to mirror those qualities in their own interactions. This chapter explores how to model respect through our actions, words, and responses, creating an environment where mutual respect thrives.
Why Modeling Respect Matters
Children learn more from what we do than from what we say. If we shout, criticize, or dismiss others, they are likely to adopt those behaviors. Conversely, when we show kindness, patience, and understanding, they internalize those values.

Respect is the foundation of all healthy relationships. Teaching it starts with:
- Self-Reflection: Being mindful of our own actions and words.
- Intentional Choices: Treating our children with the same respect we want them to show others.

Demonstrating Respectful Communication
Respectful communication is the cornerstone of gentle parenting. It shows children that their thoughts and feelings matter, even when we disagree.
1. Speak with Empathy:
- Use kind, understanding language, even during conflicts.
- ***Example***: Instead of saying, "You're being so difficult," try, "I see this is really hard for you right now."
2. Listen Actively:
- Show your child that you value their perspective by giving them your full attention.
- Avoid interrupting or dismissing their feelings, even if you don't agree.
- ***Example***: "I hear that you're upset because you wanted to keep playing. Let's talk about how we can manage our time better tomorrow."
3. Use Polite Language:
- Model phrases like "please," "thank you," and "I'm sorry" in your daily interactions.
- ***Example***: "Thank you for helping me set the table. I appreciate it."

Demonstrating Self-Regulation

Children look to us for guidance on how to handle emotions. When we model self-regulation—managing frustration, anger, or stress calmly—they learn to do the same.

1. Stay Calm in Difficult Moments:
 • When your child misbehaves or a situation becomes stressful, take a moment to breathe and respond thoughtfully instead of reacting impulsively.
 • *Example*: Instead of yelling when your child spills juice, say, "Accidents happen. Let's clean it up together."

2. Acknowledge Your Emotions:
 • Show your child that it's okay to feel emotions and that they can be managed constructively.
 • *Example*: "I'm feeling frustrated right now, so I'm going to take a deep breath before we talk."

3. Avoid Power Struggles:
 • Respect your child's autonomy while maintaining boundaries.
 • Example: "I understand you don't want to put on your shoes right now, but we need to leave soon. Would you like to put them on yourself or have me help you?"

Apologizing When You're Wrong

No one is perfect, and mistakes are a part of parenting. What matters is how we handle those moments. Apologizing to your child when you've made a mistake teaches them humility, accountability, and respect.

 • *Why It's Important:*
 • It shows your child that everyone makes mistakes, and owning up to them is a sign of strength.
 • It fosters trust and mutual respect in your relationship.

 • *How to Apologize:*
 • Be sincere and specific: "I'm sorry I yelled earlier. I was feeling overwhelmed, but that wasn't okay."
 • Avoid justifying the behavior: Focus on taking responsibility.
 • Model how to make amends: "Next time, I'll take a moment to calm down before I respond."

Practical Example: Modeling Respect in Action

One afternoon, I became frustrated when my daughter Thyri refused to clean up her toys after I asked her several times. I raised my voice, saying, "Why don't you ever listen?" Immediately, I noticed the hurt in her eyes, and I realized I hadn't handled the situation respectfully.

Here's how I repaired the moment:

1. Acknowledged My Mistake:
- I knelt down to her level and said, "I'm sorry for yelling. That wasn't respectful, and I didn't mean to hurt your feelings."

2. Explained My Feelings Calmly:
- "I was feeling frustrated because I've asked you a few times to clean up, and I need your help."

3. Modeled Problem-Solving:
- "How about we work together to clean up? You can pick up the blocks while I put away the crayons."

By apologizing and showing respect, I turned a negative moment into a learning opportunity for both of us.

Tips for Modeling Respect

- Be Mindful of Tone: How you say something matters as much as what you say. **Speak calmly and kindly.**
- Respect Their Autonomy: Allow children to make age-appropriate choices and express their opinions.
  - *Example*: "Would you like the red cup or the blue cup for your drink?"
- *Model Respect in Relationships:* Treat others—spouses, friends, or even strangers—with kindness and courtesy. Your child will notice.
- *Praise Respectful Behavior*: When your child shows respect, acknowledge it.
  - *Example*: "Thank you for saying 'please'—that was very kind."

Final Thoughts

Respect is a two-way street. By modeling respect in your words, actions, and responses, you're not only teaching your child how to treat others but also fostering a deep bond built on mutual understanding and trust.

Remember, children are always watching and learning from us. When we demonstrate empathy, self-regulation, and accountability, we show them that respect is not just something we expect—it's something we embody. By leading with respect, we create a home where kindness, understanding, and connection thrive.

Chapter 7: Creating a Harmonious Home

- **Build a Collaborative Environment**
• Involve children in family decisions (age-appropriate).
• Family meetings for discussing challenges and solutions.

Conclusion: Gentle Parenting Is a Journey
 • Gentle parenting doesn't mean perfect parenting.
 • The importance of self-care for parents.
 • Encouragement: "Every step toward gentle parenting strengthens your relationship with your child."

A harmonious home doesn't mean a home without challenges—it means a space where everyone feels valued, heard, and connected. Gentle parenting emphasizes creating an environment where empathy, respect, and boundaries guide interactions, ensuring that both parents and children feel secure and supported.
One of the most effective ways to foster harmony is to build a collaborative environment where children are involved in family decisions and feel like valued contributors. This chapter explores how to create such an environment and how tools like family meetings and shared decision-making can transform your home into a place of mutual respect and understanding.
Building a Collaborative Environment
Collaboration within the family encourages children to take ownership of their role in the household. It helps them feel included, builds their confidence, and teaches them the value of teamwork and compromise.
Involve Children in Family Decisions
When children have a voice in age-appropriate decisions, they feel empowered and respected. This doesn't mean letting children dictate everything but allowing them to contribute within reasonable boundaries.

How to Involve Children:
 1. Daily Choices:
 • Let them make small, manageable decisions.
 • *Example*: "Would you like to set the table or pour the water for dinner?"
 2. Household Rules:
 • Involve them in setting expectations for the family.
 • *Example*: "What do you think should happen if someone forgets to put away their toys?"
 3. Family Activities:
 • Give them input on weekend plans, meals, or family outings.
 • *Example*: "Do you want to go to the park or the zoo this Saturday?"
Benefits:
 • Encourages cooperation and reduces resistance.
 • Helps children feel like an important part of the family.

Family Meetings for Challenges and Solutions

Family meetings are a powerful tool for creating a harmonious home. They provide a structured space for everyone to share their thoughts, celebrate successes, and solve problems together.

How to Hold a Family Meeting:

1. Set a Regular Time:
- Choose a consistent time each week when everyone is available.

2. Create an Agenda:
- Include topics like:
- Praising good behavior or accomplishments.
- Addressing challenges (e.g., chores, schedules).
- Planning upcoming activities.

3. Encourage Participation:
- Give everyone, including younger children, a chance to speak.
- Example: "What's something you think went really well this week? What's something we could do better?"

4. Focus on Solutions:
- Approach challenges with a problem-solving mindset.
- Example: If siblings are arguing over toys, brainstorm ideas together: "What do you think is a fair way to share?"

5. Celebrate Wins:
- Acknowledge achievements, big or small, to foster a positive atmosphere.

Benefits:
- Builds communication skills and family cohesion.
- Reduces conflicts by addressing issues constructively.
- Strengthens bonds by showing that everyone's voice matters.

Conclusion: Gentle Parenting Is a Journey

Gentle parenting isn't about being perfect—it's about being intentional. Creating a harmonious home takes patience, practice, and self-compassion. There will be tough days, but each step you take toward empathy, respect, and firm boundaries strengthens your relationship with your child.

Perfection Isn't the Goal: Mistakes are part of the journey. Use them as opportunities to model accountability and growth.

Prioritize Self-Care: A harmonious home begins with a well-supported parent. Take time to recharge and care for your own emotional well-being.
- Celebrate Progress: Focus on the small victories—each moment of connection, understanding, and collaboration makes a difference.

Encouragement:

Every step you take toward gentle parenting is a step toward a stronger, more trusting relationship with your child. Trust yourself, embrace the journey, and remember that you're creating a home filled with love, respect, and growth.

Bonus
Navigating Conflict with Care

Chapter 8 Navigating Conflict with Care

- Conflict is a natural part of any relationship, including parenting.
- Healthy conflict resolution teaches children communication, empathy, and problem-solving.
- The goal isn't to avoid conflict but to manage it respectfully.

Navigating Conflict with Care: Why Conflict Is an Opportunity for Growth
Conflict is a natural part of parenting and an essential part of life. Rather than seeing conflict as a failure, gentle parenting reframes it as an opportunity for growth—for both you and your child. These moments provide a chance to teach important skills like emotional regulation, problem-solving, and empathy. By approaching conflict with care, you demonstrate how to navigate disagreements respectfully while maintaining firm boundaries. When handled thoughtfully, conflict deepens trust, strengthens the parent-child bond, and equips your child with the tools to face challenges confidently in the future. Each conflict becomes a stepping stone toward greater understanding, resilience, and connection.

1. Stay Calm and Regulate Yourself First
- Children feed off your emotional energy.
- Techniques to manage your own emotions:
- Deep breathing.
- Mental grounding exercises (e.g., "I am safe, and I can handle this").
- Pause before reacting to avoid escalating the situation.

2. Acknowledge and Validate Feelings
- Validation doesn't mean agreeing; it means showing you understand.
- Example:
- Child: "I hate you!"
- Parent: "You're really upset right now. I hear you."

3. Set Boundaries with Compassion
- It's okay to empathize while enforcing boundaries.
- Example:
- "I know you're angry, but we don't hit. Let's find another way to show how you feel."
- Use phrases like:
- "I understand, but…"
- "It's okay to feel angry, but yelling is not okay."

4. Engage in Collaborative Problem-Solving
 • Turn conflict into a teaching moment.
 • Steps for resolving conflict together:
 1. Identify the Problem Together: "What's going on? Let's talk about it."
 2. Brainstorm Solutions: Encourage the child to share their ideas.
 3. Agree on a Plan: Decide together on the best solution.
 4. Follow Up: Revisit the situation later to see if the solution worked.

5. Teach Emotional Regulation
 • Equip your child with tools to manage their emotions:
 • Calm-down spaces: A designated area with comforting items.
 • Emotion naming: Help children label feelings like frustration, sadness, or anger.
 • Breathing exercises: Teach simple techniques, like "smell the flower, blow out the candle."

6. Use Repair and Reconnection
 • Conflict can leave a rift if not addressed. Repair the relationship after resolving the issue:
 • Apologize if needed: "I'm sorry I yelled earlier. That wasn't okay."
 • Hug or reconnect through a shared activity: "Let's read a book together."

7. Teach Conflict Management Skills for Peer Interactions
 • Model and role-play situations where they can practice:
 • Taking turns speaking.
 • Using "I" statements: "I feel upset when you take my toy."
 • Finding compromises.

8. Know When to Take a Break
 • Sometimes, both you and your child may need space to cool down.
 • Use phrases like:
 • "We're both feeling upset. Let's take a few minutes and talk after we've calmed down."

Conflict Example Scenarios

Scenario 1: Sibling Argument Over a Toy
1. Validate both children's feelings: "You both want the toy, and that's frustrating."
2. Help them take turns: "Let's set a timer for 5 minutes each."
3. Teach sharing or negotiating skills: "What's a fair way to decide who gets it first?"

Scenario 2: Child Refuses to Clean Up
1. Stay calm and state the boundary: "We clean up after playtime."
2. Offer choices: "Do you want to clean up with me or by yourself?"
3. Use logical consequences: "If the toys aren't cleaned up, they'll need to take a break for tomorrow."

Empowering Parents to Stay Strong During Conflict
• Remember: Conflict doesn't mean you're failing as a parent. It's an opportunity to teach life skills.
• Prioritize connection over control while keeping boundaries firm.
• Reflect after each conflict: "What went well? What could I do differently next time?"

Certainly! Here's an additional chapter or section to include in your eBook, focusing on the importance of accepting children for who they are becoming, even when it diverges from parental expectations.

Bonus
Embracing Your Child's Unique Identity

Chapter 9 Embracing Your Child's Unique Identity

Embracing Your Child's Unique Identity: Why Acceptance Matters
Every child is born with their own unique personality, strengths, and perspective on the world. As parents, embracing your child's individuality fosters self-confidence, emotional well-being, and a secure sense of belonging. Acceptance means recognizing and celebrating who your child truly is, rather than trying to shape them to fit your expectations or societal norms. When you approach your child with empathy and respect, you create a safe space for them to explore their identity without fear of judgment. This unconditional acceptance strengthens your bond and helps them grow into their most authentic and confident selves, ready to embrace their place in the world.

Why Acceptance Matters

- Every child is unique and will grow into a person with their own strengths, preferences, and values.
- Acceptance fosters self-esteem, confidence, and a healthy parent-child relationship.
- Resisting the urge to shape your child to meet your expectations allows them to flourish authentically.

1. Reflect on Your Expectations
- Take a moment to consider what expectations you might unconsciously hold:
  - Are you projecting your unfulfilled dreams onto your child?
  - Are you trying to shape their behavior to fit societal norms or your own experiences?
- Journaling Exercise: Write down your expectations of your child and evaluate if they align with your child's natural interests, temperament, or abilities.

2. Learn to See Your Child's Strengths
- Focus on what makes your child unique:
  - Do they have a creative streak?
  - Are they naturally empathetic or inquisitive?
- Shift from criticism to encouragement by reframing challenges as opportunities for growth.
  - Example: A child who talks back may have strong self-advocacy skills.

3. Foster Individuality
 • Create an environment where your child feels free to explore their interests:
 • Let them choose activities or hobbies without imposing your preferences.
 • Celebrate their successes, even if they're not the achievements you envisioned.

4. Let Go of Comparison
 • Avoid comparing your child to their siblings, peers, or your own childhood.
 • Example: Instead of saying, "Why can't you be more like your brother?" try, "I see you're doing your best in your own way."

5. Celebrate Milestones at Their Pace
 • Each child develops differently.
 • Be patient and supportive as they meet milestones in their own time, whether it's academic achievements, social skills, or personal interests.

6. Accept Their Changing Interests and Identities
 • As children grow, their preferences, values, and identities may shift:
 • They might choose different career aspirations than you imagined.
 • They might express themselves in ways that feel unfamiliar to you (e.g., fashion, language, or identity).
 • Practice curiosity over judgment:
 • "Tell me more about why you love this."
 • "What makes you feel excited about this choice?"

7. Nurture Open Communication
 • Create a safe space where your child can express their feelings, thoughts, and dreams without fear of rejection.
 • Avoid dismissive language like, "That's silly" or "You'll change your mind." Instead, try:
 • "That sounds interesting! How did you come to feel this way?"
 • "I'd love to learn more about what excites you."

8. Respect Their Autonomy
 • As your child grows older, they'll begin making decisions for themselves.
 • Offer guidance when needed, but resist micromanaging their choices.
 • Example: "I trust you to decide what's best, but I'm here if you want advice."

9. Address Disappointments with Grace
- It's natural to feel a sense of loss when your child's path doesn't align with your expectations.
- Acknowledge those feelings privately and reframe them:
- Instead of thinking, "Why didn't they choose what I hoped?" try, "What can I learn from who they're becoming?"
- Journaling Prompt: Write about the positive aspects of your child's unique choices and identity.

10. Model Unconditional Love
- Reinforce that your love isn't tied to their achievements, choices, or how well they meet your expectations.
- Use affirming phrases:
- "I love you for who you are, not what you do."
- "You don't have to be perfect for me to be proud of you."

Example Scenarios

Scenario 1: Your Child Wants a Career You Didn't Envision
- Parent's Reaction: "I thought you'd want to be a doctor, but you're interested in art?"
- Gentle Parenting Response: "Art makes you so happy, and I can see how passionate you are. How can I support you in this?"

Scenario 2: Your Teen Expresses a New Identity
- Parent's Reaction: "This is just a phase."
- Gentle Parenting Response: "Thank you for sharing this with me. I'm here to learn and support you as you figure out who you are."

Conclusion: Loving Your Child as They Are
- Embracing your child's individuality strengthens your bond and helps them develop into a confident, self-assured adult.
- Remind yourself: Your role as a parent is to guide and love, not to mold them into your vision.
- Let go of control, trust the journey, and celebrate the person they're becoming.

Conclusion: Embracing the Parenting Journey

Parenting is an ever-evolving experience, filled with challenges, growth, and opportunities to build meaningful connections with your child. This book has walked you through the foundational principles of gentle parenting, from establishing your philosophy and building strong bonds to navigating conflict and embracing your child's unique identity.

Gentle parenting doesn't require perfection; it's about progress, patience, and prioritizing relationships over rigid expectations. By setting clear boundaries, fostering open communication, modeling respect, and learning to adapt, you create a nurturing environment where your child feels seen, valued, and empowered to thrive.

Every step you take on this journey strengthens your relationship with your child while teaching them the essential skills of empathy, resilience, and self-awareness. Parenting is as much about your growth as it is about theirs—learning to let go of control, managing your own emotions, and celebrating who they are becoming.

As you move forward, remember: You're not alone, and no parent has all the answers. Trust the process, seek joy in the little moments, and above all, love your child for who they are. The lessons shared here are just the beginning—your unique journey continues to unfold.

Thank you

Thank you for choosing to spend your valuable time with this book. Writing Not A Dr. Just A Mom was a deeply personal journey for me, and knowing that it has reached you means more than I can express.

Parenting is one of life's greatest adventures, filled with moments of joy, growth, and challenge. My hope is that the words on these pages have offered you encouragement, practical tools, and a sense of connection. If even one idea here helps you build a stronger bond with your child, then this book has fulfilled its purpose.

To every parent, caregiver, or loved one striving to nurture a child with empathy, respect, and firm boundaries—thank you for your courage, love, and dedication. Your efforts matter more than you may realize, and the impact you make will shape the future in ways that go far beyond today.

Thank you for trusting me to be a part of your parenting journey. I am deeply grateful for you.

Here's an example of how you can craft a "Notes and Reflections" page for your book:

Notes & Reflections

This space is yours to reflect on your journey as you read Not a Dr. Just A Mom. Use it to capture your thoughts, insights, and breakthroughs. Whether you're jotting down challenges, celebrating progress, or brainstorming improvements, this page is your personal canvas for growth.
- What have you learned so far about gentle parenting?
- Are there specific challenges you'd like to overcome?
- What improvements or successes have you noticed?

Write freely. There are no wrong answers here—only your unique journey.

Reflection Prompts:
- What was the most impactful idea from this chapter?
- How can I apply this lesson in my daily parenting?
- What small step can I take today to create a more empathetic, respectful environment?

Notes & Reflections

Notes & Reflections

Notes & Reflections

Notes & Reflections

Notes & Reflections

Notes & Reflections

Notes & Reflections

Notes & Reflections

Notes & Reflections

Notes & Reflections

Notes & Reflections

Notes & Reflections

Notes & Reflections

Notes & Reflections

Notes & Reflections

Notes & Reflections

Notes & Reflections

Notes & Reflections

Notes & Reflections

Notes & Reflections

Notes & Reflections

Notes & Reflections

Notes & Reflections

Notes & Reflections

Notes & Reflections

Notes & Reflections

Notes & Reflections

Notes & Reflections

Notes & Reflections

Notes & Reflections

Notes & Reflections

Notes & Reflections

Notes & Reflections

Notes & Reflections

Notes & Reflections

Notes & Reflections

Notes & Reflections

Made in United States
North Haven, CT
13 August 2025